THE WRITER'S ROADMAP

Paving the Way to Your Ideal Writing Life

LEIGH SHULMAN

ACKNOWLEDGEMENTS

This book wouldn't have been possible without support, advice and input from many people.

First, Lea Woodward. I first heard of this OGSM thing in her business mastermind all those years ago.

Thank you to Asha Rajan and Eileen Smith who read the first messy shitty first draft and also the shitty second draft of this book with great patience and care. "Every writer needs a reader," I always say. I was lucky to have them.

Another round of thank yous to Lisa Ferguson, Amanda L. Pouncy, Sandy Biback and Kathleen Evans. Their comments, time and attention smoothed the edges and brought this book to the final version you read today.

And finally, to anyone who ever thought they couldn't write. I'm here to say it's not true. You can. You will!

INTRODUCTION

Sheer desperation. That's where this book began.

For too long, I juggled family, home, work, and tried to write but never seemed to accomplish anything significant. My to-do lists resembled the multi-headed hydra more than an organization tool. As fast as I finished one task, another two sprouted in its place. Work and home tasks mingled in ever-lengthening scratchings on pieces of paper I'd copy and recopy as they became too full to add another thing.

I was working hard, yet getting nowhere. I wasn't getting better assignments. I never settled into a niche I could call expertise. I wasn't being paid properly, either, which meant I had to find other work to pay my bills. Instead of writing, I taught random classes, designed websites and felt frustrated and stuck with my non-existent writing life.

Does this sound at all familiar?

Yes, chaos is often part of being a writer. You have amazing ideas for books, articles, projects, and collaborations, but when you're spread too thin, your ideas don't come to fruition. Instead, you grapple with shapeless to-dos and murky timelines to complete as-yet unformed goals. Between writing chapters of a book, you throw a pitch into the editorial void. When not pitching, you're chasing an editor or checking on payments. Trying to balance all these disparate parts of our writing lives is dizzying. And in those moments when we feel pulled in too many directions, it is impossible to focus.

Then One Day, I Realized Something Huge

One day it hit me. I wasn't getting anywhere, because I didn't know what I wanted from my writing. A book? Yes. To publish in magazines? Sure. But there wasn't anything tying my ideas together.

It's so simple, really. If you don't know what you want, you can't outline a clear plan to get from where you are now to where you want to go.

Imagine this as a road trip. You leave New York City with no specific destination in mind. You can't know how long it will take. You don't know whether to pack a bathing suit or a heavy coat. You won't be able to budget for gas money, either.

Writing runs on the same principle.

I was frustrated with my writing career (or lack thereof) because I had absolutely no idea where I was going.

In what felt like a last ditch attempt to find some order in my writing life, I joined a women's business development group. Nothing else worked, so why not try something totally different?

My first week in the group, I learned about a business tool called an OGSM. OGSM stands for Objective, Goals, Strategies and Measures. It's a short form business plan used by small business owners to define goals and map out short and long term targets. It eases communication between team members, so people can work together more efficiently and effectively.

I could not believe how well it worked for me. Within a month of creating my first OGSM, I started a writing mastermind group, began taking one-on-one clients, and published five new articles. Since then, my OGSM has guided me to accomplish things I barely believed possible in my pre-OGSM life.

I founded Creative Revolution international writing retreats for women writing books. I launched The Workshop, my online writing academy to build writing skills, find your community, and learn to be paid for your words.

Now, I write, travel, and spend my time coaching women one-on-one and at inspirational retreats because I want to help more women feel confident with their writing, finish their masterpieces and be exactly the kind of writers they've always dreamed of being.

My work has been featured in publications such as The Washington Post, The New York Times, The Guardian, Guernica, and many others. Plus, I'm working on my third book, a YA novel I began during National Novel Writing Month.

Now it's your turn to stop struggling and decide exactly what you want from your writing so you can make your writing dreams come true.

Breaking Down The OGSM

There are four separate parts to an OGSM. Together, they create a clear Objective for your writing then pave the way from where you are now to where you want to go.

If you remember, those four letters stand for Objective, Goals, Strategies and Measures. Let's look at what each means.

If an OGSM were a road trip, the Objective would be your final destination. The Objective outlines what you want from your writing and how it fits into the bigger picture of your career and life.

We'll spend more time on your Objective than any other part of the plan because to achieve your dreams, you have to know what they are. **The simple act of knowing what you want empowers you.** Your Objective, when properly constructed, will guide you for years to come. You won't need to go back and change it often.

Then each successive step -- Goals, Strategies, and Measures -- breaks your Objective into manageable and actionable parts.

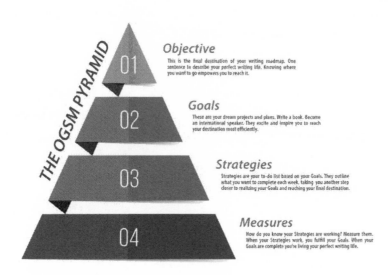

THE OGSM PYRAMID

01 Objective
This is the final destination of your writing roadmap. One sentence to describe your perfect writing life. Knowing where you want to go empowers you to reach it.

02 Goals
These are your dream projects and plans. Write a book. Become an international speaker. They excite and inspire you to reach your destination most efficiently.

03 Strategies
Strategies are your to-do list based on your Goals. They outline what you want to complete each week, taking you another step closer to realizing your Goals and reaching your final destination.

04 Measures
How do you know your Strategies are working? Measure them. When your Strategies work, you fulfill your Goals. When your Goals are complete you're living your perfect writing life.

Your Goals are your dream ideas and projects. Goals give you a general idea of what you'd like to do while on your road trip. It's what you imagine your road trip will be before you start planning any of the details. There's wind in your face as you drive down the road. You stop to take photos of a gorgeous view or eat foods that are the specialty of that locale. It's exciting but still fuzzy on specifics.

Most of us get stuck on Goals when we think of our ideal writing life. We know we want to write books or publish in our favorite magazines, but we don't yet know how to accomplish these things.

Strategies start to fill in the how-to of your Goals. On your road trip, they are the specific towns you'll visit, the things you'll eat, and the attractions that make you pull over to the side of the road. In your writing life, Strategies are the to-do building blocks, the actionable steps that allow you to make your Goals a reality.

Finally, Measures are the ways you quantify each Strategy to evaluate whether or not it's working for you. This is how many pitches you send, how many pages you write, and how much money you make when publishing. Once we've created the rest of your OGSM plan, we'll talk about how Measures allow you to determine whether or not your Strategies are working.

To realize your writing plan, you begin with the M and work backwards. When you've achieved your Measures, you've completed your Strategies. When your Strategies are in place, you've met your Goals. And when you've fulfilled your Goals, you are living Your Life's Objective.

What The OGSM Did For Me & What This Book Will Do For You

This method worked miracles for me.

I knew I wanted to write and teach, but I didn't know what that looked like in real life. My OGSM helped me consciously design the life I wanted. I began to recognize what was working for me and what wasn't. I quit jobs that didn't fit into my OGSM and let people know they could hire me to mentor them in writing. As I taught more, I phased out low-paying jobs that took up too much time and had nothing to do with writing.

Suddenly, I had more time to write, so I threw myself into pitching editors. I sketched out ideas for a book or two (this one included). Best of all, I was paid for my work, so writing and teaching became a viable way to pay my bills.

Here I am, eight years after my very first OGSM, doing exactly what I always dreamed of doing. I write and publish books and articles. My teaching allows me to travel as I host international writing retreats. I spend my days writing, teaching and working with other women helping them achieve their writing dreams.

My own OGSM so transformed the way I manage my writing I knew I had to adapt this business tool for writers. Since then, I've used the OGSM method with hundreds of clients in my classes and one-on-ones. I've had the distinct pleasure of watching them write books, become recognized experts in their fields, and even leave careers they no longer wanted to carve out the creative space they need to make a full-time living writing.

Now it's your turn!

How To Use This Book

In this workbook, we'll complete a series of exercises designed to work through each section of the OGSM one letter at a time. You'll also find scratch pages right here in this book for you to keep your notes and write the exercises.

I suggest completing these exercises over the course of two or three days. Wait a bit between exercises to give your ideas a chance to marinate; but not too long. A few hours is useful, any more than a day per question and you're procrastinating.

In these exercises, you'll brainstorm to generate ideas, mind-map to form connections between those ideas, and freewrite to move past the fear that causes you to freeze up and forget what you really want.

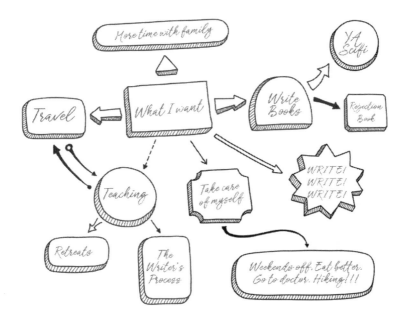

You'll start by envisioning the ideal life you want for your writing. Maybe that means writing that book you've always wanted to write. Or publishing articles related to your current interests. Or carving space for your writing while maintaining a career you love and don't want to leave. Or quit your job to write full time. Maybe something else entirely.

Believe me when I tell you anything is possible!

Over the course of the first chapter, I'll offer ways to shape your Objective so it truly reflects your ideal writing life. Then we'll break your Objective into manageable pieces you'll prioritize and quantify. Finally, we'll create a plan so you can accomplish each piece.

Step by step, you will see your writing dream become a reality.

The first time you work through the exercises in this book, you'll create your initial writing roadmap. But your needs and abilities will change over time. That's why I designed this workbook to be a touchstone you can revisit month after month, year after year, to stay on track with your Objective as you learn more, know more, and create more.

Throughout this book, I offer plenty of real-life client examples for each section of the OGSM as well as share my own OGSM to help guide you as you design your own path.

Then, once you have all your ideas laid out in front of you, we'll focus on creating a crystal clear plan including where you want to live, what you want to do, and where you'd like to see yourself in one, two, or five years down the line.

As your writing grows, your OGSM grows with you.

Why Use A Business Tool For A Creative Endeavor Like Writing?

When you have a concrete plan, you can ignore all the distractions and plot a path for yourself. When you treat your writing as a business, you can set yourself up properly in a world that increasingly calls on writers to build platforms, create brands, and market ourselves.

If you think this all sounds great, but you're not sure it will work for you, know it's natural to feel that way at the beginning. Just remind yourself you're building your writing one step at a time, and it all starts with a clear one sentence Objective to guide everything you do. Ready to get started? Let's do this!

O IS FOR OBJECTIVE

FINDING YOUR DESIRE AND PURPOSE IN LIFE

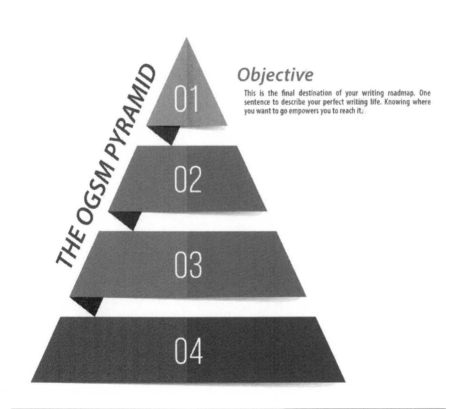

THE OGSM PYRAMID

01

Objective

This is the final destination of your writing roadmap. One sentence to describe your perfect writing life. Knowing where you want to go empowers you to reach it.

02

03

04

Want to know the #1 reason people don't achieve their purpose in life? The answer is surprisingly simple.

They don't know what they want.

If you don't know what you want, how can you possibly hope to accomplish it?

Imagine going on a road trip. You lock the door to your house, jump in the car, and just start driving aimlessly. Sure, that could be exciting for a while, but at some point, you'll want to do something. You'll get hungry. You'll get bored of driving. If you didn't pack the right shoes and have no money for a hot dog, you won't be able to take advantage of the opportunities along the way. Lack of preparation forces you to backtrack, repeat steps, and may even leave you stranded and lost.

Your Objective is the final destination of your writer's roadmap. It's the guiding star that pulls together every other part of your plan. That's why we'll spend more time carefully crafting the Objective than any other part of your OGSM. We want to make sure it includes details that reflect your work, your home life, and also the core values that make you who you are.

Can you picture your writing life? Do you see the type of projects you most want to write? Can you imagine your view when you look out the window from your writing desk? Can you see yourself making careful choices for your career that support the writing life you want to create?

If not, don't worry, you will soon.

For many writers, self-doubt and self-criticism get in the way of knowing what they want. You second guess yourself and worry you couldn't possibly accomplish your writing dream. You wonder if you're talented enough. Will anyone even want to read what you have to say? Too often, well-meaning friends and family add pressure to this stew pot with their misplaced questions and expectations.

That's why it's crucial to have a straightforward, well-defined description of exactly what you want to do in your writing life.

Once your Objective is in place, you'll see the other pieces fall quickly into order.

What Is An Objective?

If I asked you to describe your dream writing life, what would you say?

Your Objective combines all of your ideas and desires into one sentence. That one sentence is incredibly powerful as it lays out your path, your direction, and gives you the information you need to plan stops along the way.

A HOW-TO CHECKLIST FOR YOUR OBJECTIVE

1. Keep It Short

When someone asks where you're going for vacation, you probably tell them something straightforward like "We're driving to San Francisco." You're unlikely to recount the myriad ways to get there or explain how road signs work. Similarly, one sentence is enough for your Objective. You want a succinct statement that includes your most important points. When you try to include too much, you end up losing focus.

> NOTE: If you use a lot of "ands" in your sentence, you're probably pushing too many pieces together.

For example:

Not this: I want to self-publish children's stories after I find an agent. I'll illustrate the books myself and live near my parents and siblings so I can visit them for holidays.

But this: I want to get past my fears so I have enough time to write children's stories that I illustrate myself and keep my nursing career.

2. Keep it general

When driving to San Francisco, you leave your house with your car keys, money and a general idea of what you'd like to see along the way. You don't need to know the exact location of each stop or what you'll eat for breakfast next Tuesday.

By keeping your Objective broad, you guard it against becoming obsolete.

Think of it this way; if your Objective includes writing the sci-fi YA novel that's been bumping around your brain, you'll have to change your Objective once you finish writing the book. If instead, your Objective states you want to Write Books, you leave room for much more flexibility in your thinking and planning.

> *Your Objective, when constructed well, will change little over time. I've used the same one for the last five years. I don't have any need to change it soon, either.*

More Objective Examples:

Not this: I want to write and publish a series of adventure YA novels, do freelance writing for adventure travel magazines, and share my fiction in literary journals, plus speak at bookstores and universities about how-to become a writer.

But This: I want to make my living writing, selling books, and inspirational speaking while working from anywhere.

Not this: I want to publish a series of YA novels with black main characters as well as write articles that will help me sell books and earn money. Plus help mentor women like me as they write their books.

But this: I want to found a publishing company to publish my own writing as well as writing from young women of color who don't have the confidence in their writing and characters.

Not this: I want to write about parenting but also take advantage of my years of working before I became a stay-at-home-mom and make enough time to still spend with my family.

But this: I want to build a business that allows me enough free time to write about parenting, my own life experiences, finances and marketing.

3. Include elements outside your work life

While the main purpose of an OGSM is to guide your work life, it's also designed to make room for your personal life, hobbies, family, and anything else that makes your life enjoyable, relaxed, and fun.

Keep your personal life in mind when constructing your plan, too. Your Objective can include family, where you live, and the things you love doing when you're not working.

OGSM examples that include non-work related

Not this: I want to write novels.

But this: I want to travel regularly while I write novels and visit my family and friends around the world.

Not this: I want to be a freelance writer.

But this: I want to write and publish articles for magazines and businesses that allow me to focus on fitness and eating healthfully.

4. Your Objective includes words that reflect your core values.

"What are core values?" you ask.

These are the people, places, things, and emotions that define you and your beliefs. They help distinguish your plan from other Objectives by including the things that are most important to you.

They can include everything from areas of expertise such as education, travel, or photography to the feelings and ethics that guide your life, such as love, energy, or charity.

Don't worry too much about including your core values right now. We'll discuss them and the role they play at the end of this section, once you have a clearer idea of what your Objective will be.

This is a lot of weight for just one sentence to carry, but it's easier than you think to pin down. The following exercises help you tap into your unconscious thoughts and desires about yourself and your work. You'll be amazed at how quickly what you want comes into focus.

Let's jump directly into the exercises now!

OBJECTIVE: FINDING YOUR DESIRE AND PURPOSE WORKSHEETS

Over the next pages, I'll ask you to answer three questions and complete one writing exercise. Each is designed to help you get past your doubt and tap into what you really want. Each question builds on the previous one, so it's important you do them in the order presented here.

For each question, I'd like you to free write your answers. Free writing has a particular structure and method. Let me explain.

What Is Free Writing?

For each of the three questions, you'll need a timer and a pen and paper or a journal. Or if you prefer typing on a computer, open a new document. Write in whatever way works best for you.

Before you begin writing your responses to each question, set your timer for 10 or 15 minutes.

The only rules:
- No erasing.
- No crossing out.
- No editing.
- No stopping to ponder or second guess yourself.

Just write.

If the thoughts that surface make no sense or don't seem to have anything to do with your writing goals, write them down anyway. If you think the exercise is stupid or you have nothing to say, write it down.

If you reach the end of a particular train of thought or you're bored and don't want to continue, just move on to the next line and keep going with the next topic.

It may feel uncomfortable, but I promise, this is an exercise I've done in hundreds of classes and one-on-ones over twenty years of teaching. It works.

Now, it's time for you to start free writing your answer the first of the three questions.

Question One

Set your timer for ten minutes and free write your answers to the following question:

WHEN YOU PICTURE YOUR IDEAL WRITING LIFE, WHAT DOES IT INCLUDE?

Don't worry about whether you're qualified or what resources you might need to make it happen. If you feel any fear or anxiety pop up, acknowledge it briefly and keep going. The only thing you have to do right now is focus on what you want.

Go big. Go bold. Go blue sky.

Don't let anything hold you back from what you imagine and dream.

Pro-Tip: Go Blue Sky with your Goals

What do I mean by blue sky?

It's a phrase people in corporate settings know well and is used in finance to refer to the best case scenario. When I say it, I mean to allow yourself to stretch to the fullest extent of your creative vision. Let yourself dream, unconstrained by what others say is realistic, possible, or practical.

Don't hold yourself back!

I've worked with thousands of writers over the last twenty years and watched as clients publish in their dream publications, free themselves of full-time jobs to freelance, and go from sitting behind a desk to traveling full time with their families. I've seen people divest themselves of debt and start making a comfortable living doing the things that inspire them.

Each of them began with an Objective that felt beyond their reach. It felt too big and too much.

Then they did it anyway!

Is possible for you? Yes. Absolutely. You'll have to work hard and put in consistent effort. You'll face setbacks. We all do. As long as you keep following your plan, you will see your Objective take root in your life.

- YOUR ANSWERS HERE -

- YOUR ANSWERS HERE –

- YOUR ANSWERS HERE -

Question Two

Now, set your timer for another ten minutes. The same rules apply. Free write without stopping and without judging what you write.

WHEN YOU PICTURE YOUR DREAM LIFE, WHAT ARE YOU DOING?

Where do you live? Who is with you?

Are you traveling full time or living in a foreign country? Maybe you'd prefer to move back to your hometown and be close to high school friends. Are you in a relationship? Do you prefer to spend time on your own?

Related to work: Do you love your job and can't imagine leaving? Or are you ready to quit and do something else? Do you need a job to pay your bills or you have enough income for now?

In that life, what do you enjoy doing? Cooking, making model airplanes, visiting cemeteries, running marathons.

Include the things you love doing and the things you want to start doing. They can be serious endeavors or flighty fun things or anything in between.

As I mentioned above, you also want to keep your personal life in mind when writing your Objective. Your work goals should leave the space and time you need to enjoy your personal pursuits.

Do you love to travel hike, dragon boat, learn new things or want to go to Burning Man for the first time? Do you have a family? Do you prefer to remain child-free? Are you happy to live out of a backpack on a limited budget with the flexibility to go where you want whenever you want?

If it's important to you, this is the place to include it.

Go ahead and write for ten or fifteen minutes. I'll be here when you get back.

- YOUR ANSWERS HERE -

- YOUR ANSWERS HERE -

- YOUR ANSWERS HERE -

Question Three

Here we are at the final question for this part of the workbook. You're doing fantastically. Keep going.

Reset your timer for another ten minutes and answer the following question:

WHAT PARTS OF YOUR LIFE NO LONGER SERVE YOU OR TAKE AWAY FROM THAT BLUE SKY PICTURE YOU'RE IMAGINING?

Now, it's time to take stock of what you're currently experiencing that you no longer want; people, jobs, places you visit or live, projects you've undertaken, promises you've made to yourself and other people.

Are these things tedious, tiring, or not worth your time?

Maybe you're just not that into them and would rather fill that space in your life with something else.

Don't worry just yet about how you can rid yourself of these things. Simply acknowledge they're no longer for you by writing them down. We'll come back to them later.

- YOUR ANSWERS HERE -

- YOUR ANSWERS HERE -

Turning The Three Free Writing Exercises Into Your One Sentence

Now that you've fleshed out your ideas on paper, we're going to take all those thoughts from your free writes and distill them into a one sentence Objective.

Take a moment to reread what you've written so far. Highlight passages or words that resonate with you. Take what you've written and create one sentence that represents the type writing life you most want to live.

Remember the checklist I included earlier:

- Keep it short.
- Keep it general.
- Include non-work elements in your life
- Incorporate your core values.

Write your one sentence now.

Feel free to try a few versions of this first Objective. Don't worry if it feels wrong or uncomfortable. We all have to start somewhere.

Once you have this first draft sentence on paper, we'll work on polishing it in the next section.

- YOUR ANSWERS HERE -

- YOUR ANSWERS HERE -

- YOUR ANSWERS HERE -

Polishing Your Objective Until It Shines

In this section, we're going to evaluate and edit your Objective until it clearly reflects the writing life you want to live.

First, let's take a look at some other examples and talk about ways you can clarify yours. I'll start with my own.

My current Objective:

> *"I want to have travel and have fun with my family while building a writing and education business that inspires and empowers women to write."*

I include fun and family first in part because they're most important to me. I know myself well enough, though, to recognize as important as my family is, I have a tendency to throw myself into my work, forgetting to come up for air. Doing so leaves me stressed, upset, and less able to focus on my work. I mention family and fun early in my Objective as a reminder to maintain a better balance.

You'll also notice I've defined the type of work I do briefly and succinctly; *Writing and education.* These three words encompass everything I do.

The education side covers my international writing retreats, webinars, one-on-one client meetings and The Workshop, my online academy for people who want to make a living with their words.

Writing covers the rest of what I do. Researched articles, personal essays, books, and even this workbook you're reading now.

These three words are general enough to include anything else I've done and most things I'd like to do one day.

If for some reason, something completely different arises, I can always tweak my Objective.

I also define my audience. I work primarily with women, so I like to state that in my Objective, to guide me as I decide on my Goals and Strategies.

Finally, I love to travel. Instead of relegating travel to a pile of one-day-I'll-do-it, I organized a career that allows me to work from anywhere. I also created projects that include travel. Often, my family comes with me, and we explore the world together.

Some other Objective examples from clients:

- I want to build a publishing and education business that allows me to live near my extended family and empowers people to express themselves creatively and achieve what they most want in life.
- I want to make my living writing, selling books, and speaking as an expert in adventure travel.
- I want to build a location independent writing business selling editing and writing software products.
- I want to get past my fears so I have enough time to write children's stories that I illustrate myself and keep my nursing career.
- I want to write meaningful fiction that fulfills my desire for creativity while also allowing me to pay half my bills with writing.

Each of these clients, by the way, achieved the life he or she envisioned when we first began working together. I've seen it happen over and over. Just as the clients who wrote the above Objectives created their ideal writing lives, so can you.

Now It's Your Turn

Now, let's evaluate the Objective you just wrote according to the checklist I gave you earlier in this chapter.

Keep it short.

Is your Objective one clear sentence? Have you kept your ands and buts to a minimum? Also, is it truly one sentence and not a few spliced together with punctuation?

If you answered yes to these questions, great. If not, go back and modify your Objective until it is one succinct and clear sentence.

Keep it general

Have you included details such as publishing dates, books you'll write, places you'd like to pitch where you'd like to work, or with whom you'd like to collaborate? Do you discuss the how, when, where, why, and who of your plan?

If you have too many specifics, go back and edit them out, keeping your Objective as wide ranging as possible.

Include non-work related elements in your Objective

Does your OGSM have at least one detail that focuses on your life outside of your writing and work?
If not, decide what parts of your non-work life are most important to you. Family. Freedom. Travel. Ability to live anywhere. Time to relax.

Then, go back and revise your Objective to include one or more of these things.

Incorporate your core values

"What are core values," you ask, and what are they doing in your business and writing plan?

Core values define you and the choices you make. They can be people, places, descriptives, emotions, or anything that makes your OGSM personal to you and your beliefs and values.

Words like inspire, create, and connect represent the type of impact you have on others and the world around you.

Educate, write, and organize describe the type of work you want to do.

Integrity, flexibility, and stability reflect the qualities you want in your life.

What words and phrases best reflect who you are?

EMPOWER, BUILD, TEACH, LEAD, FUN, FREEDOM, TRAVEL, ACCOMPLISH, DESIGN, COMMUNITY, DEVELOP, EXPRESS, EMOTION, CONSISTENT, SELL, DRAW, PHOTOGRAPH, GLOBAL, LOCAL, POWERFUL, IMPACTFUL, SUCCESSFUL, WHERE I WANT, HOW I WANT, WITH WHOM I WANT, VALUABLE, BENEFIT, LEARNS, POWERFUL, FOOD, CALM, CONFIDENT, ENERGETIC, HAPPY, HELPFUL, BEAUTY, MATURE, YOUTHFUL, TRUTH, DILIGENT, BALANCE, HONEST, OPEN-MINDED, EXAMINE, RESPECTFUL, NURTURING, IDEAS, INFORMATION, INSTANTLY, OVER TIME, COLLABORATION, INTEGRATION, BELIEF, DIVERSITY. INTEGRITY, FLEXIBILITY, CHANGE, STABILITY, BUILD

If you use words that aren't on the word cloud above; No problem. Your core values are unique to you.

Going back to some earlier examples of Objective, we can highlight the core values and see the role they play in shaping your OGSM.

- I want to build a **publishing** and **education** business that allows me to live near **my extended family** and **empowers** people to express themselves **creatively** and **achieve** what they most want in life.
- I want to **make a living** writing, selling books, and speaking as an **expert** in **adventure travel**.
- I want to build a **location independent** writing business selling editing and writing software products.
- I want to **get past my fears** so I have **enough time** to write **children's stories** that I **illustrate** myself and keep my **nursing** career.
- I want to write **meaningful** fiction that fulfills my **desire for creativity** while also allowing me to **pay half my bills** with writing.
- And of course, my own Objective presents my core values front and center.
- I want to have **travel** and **have fun** with my **family** while building a **writing** and **education** business that **inspires** and **empowers women** to write.

Read through your own Objective and see what core values you've included. Do they highlight your ethics? Do they inspire you? Do they make you feel good about the life you'll be living once you implement your OGSM?

Go back and make changes as you see fit. When you're ready, we'll move to the final Objective exercise.

- YOUR ANSWERS HERE -

A List Of Questions To Evaluate Your Objective

Ask yourself the following questions now that you have your core values in place:

> Does your one sentence overview paint a vision of your ideal life?
> Are you excited about this career you're going to create?
> Do the words you've chosen to describe your career and life appeal to you?
> Do they reflect the kind of person you are and want to be?
> Do they reflect your deepest held values?
> Does it create a clear picture of the kind of work you will do?
> Do you include non-work-related elements?

If you answered yes to these questions, well done. If not, what do you need to change, remove, or add to make it match your ideal?

It's likely you'll still have questions and doubts about this first Objective of yours. My first ever road trip was far from optimal. I got lost and had to reroute back on track. I ran into a snowbank somewhere in Ohio and had to call the police for a tow. (No joke!)

That's ok. You have to start somewhere.

As you implement your initial OGSM in real life, you'll see what works and what doesn't. Understanding what you need to do to change your Objective will become second nature.

Most of all, trust yourself. You can make changes later, but for now, trust that this starting point is more than enough to get you well on the way to your ideal writing life.

Now that you've got your Objective in place, it's time to talk Goals.

G IS FOR GOALS

ALL YOUR DREAM PROJECTS IN ONE PLACE.

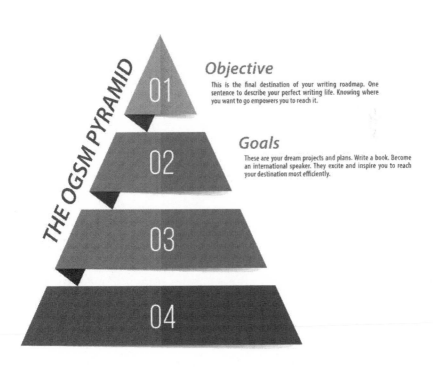

THE OGSM PYRAMID

01

Objective
This is the final destination of your writing roadmap. One sentence to describe your perfect writing life. Knowing where you want to go empowers you to reach it.

02

Goals
These are your dream projects and plans. Write a book. Become an international speaker. They excite and inspire you to reach your destination most efficiently.

03

04

In the Objectives section, you created a clear image of your ideal writing life. How does it feel to know exactly what you want?

Relieved. Thrilled. Calm. Relaxed. Determined. Inspired and motivated.

These are only some of the ways people describe how they feel once they finally put those random thoughts and ideas down on paper and organized into one clear sentence.

Now that you know what you want, we're going to see how all those ideas you have for books, courses, articles, and whatever else you've imagined doing fit into your OGSM.

Goals, simply explained, are your big plans that will make your Objective a reality.

When you plan your road trip across country, you have endless options of things to do. You can hike, eat good food, experience art and music, or enjoy kitsch. You can learn about local culture or see the wildlife, but you can't do everything at once. You must make choices.

You may love the idea of skiing in Colorado, then a visit to the Gilcrease Museum in Tulsa, followed by sloppy joes at Joe's Diner in Reno, before popping up to Canada for poutine and hiking, but the route makes absolutely no sense. Were you to follow such a circuitous route, you may never reach San Francisco.

Likewise, your Goals set you in the direction of your Objective, and thus the choices you make keep you on the most direct path. Goals are more specific than your Objective, but you won't dive into the details yet. You still want to keep them relatively general to allow room for flexibility.

The following examples from my clients illustrate what I mean:

Not this: I want to self-publish four books and then sell them via Amazon and BookBaby.

But this: I want to self-publish novels and sell them online.

Not This: I want to pitch twenty new editors a month and publish in one new magazine a month to make my living.

But This: I want to support myself entirely with freelance writing.

Not This: I'm going to run dog training clinics and meet with dog trainers with children to see how training dogs can help parents.

But This: I want to be known as an expert in dog training, child development, and the connection between these two.

Let's go back to my own OGSM to show you how I developed my Goals and how they work for me.

My Objective:

> *I want to travel and have fun with my family while building a writing and education business that inspires and empowers women to write.*

My top three goals are:
- **Write** books and articles, both fiction and non-fiction.
- **Develop** writing education products and services for women writers.
- **Establish** myself as an expert in writing, education, parenting, travel, and the intersection of these things.

They are all short, to the point statements that deepen my understanding of the type of work I mention in the Objective.

Each one leaves plenty of room to decide how I will accomplish these things.

Keeping the Goals broad and without specifics allows your OGSM to grow with you. Just as I rarely change my Objective, my Goals have remained mostly the same over the past 5 years as well.

NOW LET'S TALK ABOUT YOUR GOALS

We'll begin by focusing on the whats, whens, hows, and whys I told you to overlook in the Objective section.

What kinds of writing do you want to do?
Will you write books or are you more interested in writing shorter pieces? Or both?
How much money do you want to make?
What are your areas of expertise?
By when do you want to finish your book?
How will you sell your writing?
For what kinds of publications do you want to write?

To answer these questions and further define your Goals, we're going to work through another three part writing exercise.

Get your writing tools and timer ready.

GETTING YOUR GOALS OUT OF YOUR HEAD AND ORGANIZED ONTO PAPER

In this first exercise, we're going to brainstorm a list of all your possible responsibilities and projects. Include things you have to do, things you want to do, things you've considered doing but don't think you can, and any other ideas you've had that interest you.

Once they're all in a list in front of you, we'll prioritize and organize them. You'll decide which of these responsibilities and projects you want to do, which will go on the back burner, and which things you'll cut out of your plan entirely.

As with the writing exercises for your Objective, you're going to free write your thoughts for this exercise.

Free Write to Uncover Your Goals

Get a timer and a pen and paper or a journal. If you prefer typing on computer, open a new document. Write in whatever way works best for you.

Set your timer for 10 or 15 minutes and write down what comes to mind.

The only rules: No erasing. No crossing out. No stopping to ponder or second guess yourself.

You're not chasing perfection. Just write.

Part One of the Goals Exercise: Putting all your ideas in one place

WRITE A LIST OF ALL YOUR CURRENT PROJECTS AND RESPONSIBILITIES PLUS ALL THE PROJECT IDEAS YOU WANT TO DO OR HAVE DREAMED ABOUT DOING.

You should include:

- Everything you're working on right now even if it's not writing related.
- The great ideas you've had on the back burner but haven't had a chance to start.
- Things you've started but never finished.
- Anything else that comes to mind.

Yes, this exercise could take much longer than fifteen minutes. I've had people tell me they'd need weeks to jot down every idea.

For today, we're going to take 15 minutes to get started.

Remember, your OGSM is designed to grow with you. Any projects you forget during this 15 minutes of writing, you can incorporate later. As you have new ideas, you'll add them. As you gain more experience and learn what works for you and what doesn't, you'll modify accordingly.

Your OGSM is flexible enough to expand and change as you need it, so it doesn't matter if you don't include every single detail right this minute.

Ok, now set your timer for 15 minutes and write your list. We'll move on to the second part when you're finished.

- YOUR ANSWERS HERE -

- YOUR ANSWERS HERE -

Part Two of the Goals Exercise: Organizing your ideas.

NOW THAT YOU HAVE YOUR LIST OF EVERYTHING YOU HAVE TO DO, WANT TO DO, AND DREAM OF DOING, GO THROUGH AND SEPARATE IT INTO TWO CATEGORIES.

Category One: The things you want to continue doing or things you'd like to start doing.

Put this list aside for now, but keep it somewhere you'll find it easily. We're going to use it again to fine tune your Goals in a bit.

Category Two: List the things you don't want to do anymore.

You dread them. They're a chore, but somehow they've ended up taking time and space in your life.

Why are you still doing these things if you dislike them so much?

For many, the answer is simple. We work because we need to pay bills.

People often tell me how much they'd love to write full time, but they can't leave their jobs without another source of income. Others want to transition into writing from full-time jobs and careers but don't know how to shift their income into freelancing or publishing books. We'll discuss ways to phase out work you no longer want to do and replace it with things that excite you later in the Strategies section, too.

But you need to make a living. You can't just stop work, so leave these unwanted money making activities on your list of current projects for now.

What about the other things on your list you no longer want to do?

This can include volunteer work, activities related to your kids or your partner, or hobbies you once loved but are no longer worth your time.

Are they part of your to-do list out of obligation? Out of guilt? Habit? Or some other reason entirely.

Be honest with yourself.

If you're not receiving payment, enjoyment or any other benefit, it's time to cut these things out. That means setting boundaries.

You can rid yourself of some of these unwanted to-dos with a simple e-mail or phone call. Others may require a sit down to say to say "No, I won't be doing that anymore."

Once you've highlighted everything you plan to cut out, set aside some time to make those calls and have those talks. The second they're off your to-do list, you'll have more time and space for what you really want.

- YOUR ANSWERS HERE -

- YOUR ANSWERS HERE -

- YOUR ANSWERS HERE -

Part Three of the Goals Exercise: Identifying Your Top Three

In the second part of this exercise, you created a list of all the projects you want to do and those you must continue doing. Pick that list up again now.

READ THROUGH THE ITEMS, AND THIS TIME, YOU'RE GOING TO SEPARATE THEM INTO "TYPES" OR CATEGORIES OF PROJECTS.

The following is a list of categories you might use for your writing plan:

- Books to write
- Articles to write
- Products you've created or want to create
- Services you provide or want to develop
- Speaking engagements
- Areas of expertise
- Developing a writer's platform
- Work you do only because it helps you pay your bills (Again, we'll address how to transition out of these jobs to more fulfilling work soon.)

You may have additional categories in your list, so feel free to label them in the way that makes the most sense to you.

> *Keep your list of categories with the corresponding projects handy. We're going to use them later in the Strategies section of this book.*

Now that you have your categories, **which are your top three**?

Which three best support your Objective? Which do you most want to do? Which ones fill you with anticipation? If you could spend the rest of your days working on just three of these categories, which would you choose?

These top three categories are your Goals!

Congratulations! You've just filled in the G of your OGSM!

Why Only Three Goals?

If you're anything like me and my clients, you'll have many more categories and projects than just your three top goals. You'll probably also want to tackle everything at the same time.

I warn you now. Don't do it.

Triumvirates and trilogies abound in religion and literature. Brahma, Vishnu, Shiva, the Holy Trinity, three bears, three Fates, and three Muses. Three is a symbol of permanence in the Old Testament. And let's not forget the writing rule of three, which states things are funnier, more satisfying and more effective in groups of, yes, once again, three. We see three everywhere.

Going beyond symbolism, the human brain can grasp only so many ideas at once. After that, we become overwhelmed and stop retaining information. According to a study from the University of Oregon, our brains don't hold memories and events beyond four at a time.

Simplify your life and give yourself an edge to succeed by focusing on only three Goals at a time. You'll be more likely to focus and finish your projects, which in turn leads you more quickly to your Objective. Plus, these are the three things that excite you most, so you'll spend your time writing what you love! Total bonus!

Anything that doesn't fall into the top three of your Goals list? Forget about them. They will wait patiently on until you're ready for them.

Exceptions To The Three Goals Rule

Exception One: You're writing a book

A book takes concerted time, attention, and focus, and few people have the headspace to multitask while writing one. When you try to squeeze it into a larger plan that includes too many other projects, your book will sink to the bottom of your to-do list, where it languishes. I see this happen often as people include "Write a book" in their Goals, but it's the last item on the list. Unsurprisingly, people rarely move past their first Goals to write their books.

Give your book and yourself some breathing room.

If at all possible, let writing your book be your only writing goal during that time. Or focus on two goals, no more.

Client Case Study:

I completed a novel with a woman who worked for many years as an occupational therapist for students with autism. Her husband worked full time and made enough money to support them. They decided together for her to take a year off and work on her novel about a family struggling to understand their son's diagnosis of autism. She wrote and finished her book. Then what did she do?

Many writers report feeling incredibly lost when they finish writing a book. It makes sense, too. You've just spent months, years even, immersed in a world of your own creation. Then, suddenly, it's over. While you'll obviously be elated you've accomplished something so huge, you'll also be left wondering what to do next.

Your OGSM once again provides the structure you need to move forward.

Once this client completed her book, she returned to the list of projects she generated during her Goals exercise and chose her next three projects.

- Becoming an expert in her field.
- Freelance writing.
- Publishing her finished book.

She started writing freelance articles on subjects related to her novel which were based on her previous work as a therapist. This established her as an expert in the field and also helped her develop her audience for her soon-to-be-published book. She started an e-mail newsletter for people who wanted to know more about her work which she used to market the book and generate sales once it published. All that, and she also gained income from her freelancing and book sales.

Most of us can't stop everything else for a book. We have jobs, family, and other responsibilities that need our attention. If your job requires writing, it can be a struggle to finish work for the day only to pick up your pen again to write your book. Even more reason to make careful choices and not spread yourself thin with too many Goals.

Exception Two: When you're transitioning from your full-time job or career to writing full time.

I've been promising to talk about how your full-time job -- or any work you no longer want to do -- fits into your OGSM.

Now is the time.

It's not a revelation to say working full or part-time requires a huge portion of our energy. Even so, many writers forget to include their jobs as a Goal when they design their OGSMs.

I suggest including "Transition from current job to full time writing" as one of your three Goals. As you work through the next steps in your OGSM, you'll create Strategies to replace your current job's income with writing work until you can leave your job entirely.

As your income from other sources grows, you'll see how and when you no longer need your current work.

The Metrics Of Dates And Dollar Amounts: Why Do We Need Them?

While it's not absolutely necessary to include dates and amounts, I suggest including them anyway. These metrics keep you accountable to your plans.

Some examples of Goals from previous clients that include money and dates:

- I want to write a novel and have it ready to send to agents by [DATE.]
- I want to be a paid speaker as an expert in dog care and plant biology making [AMOUNT OF MONEY]
- I want to earn [AMOUNT OF MONEY]/year publishing freelance articles both in print and online.
- I want to develop a for-pay online support group for people looking to break into copyediting. [AMOUNT OF MONEY}
- I want to earn [AMOUNT OF MONEY]/year on my freelance writing by [DATE]
- I want to phase out my current job and replace that [AMOUNT OF MONEY} income with writing jobs by [DATE].

Many people feel incredibly uncomfortable setting these numbers. You may feel it as well. Self-doubt creeps into your head, whispering "How is that ever going to happen? That's too soon. That's too much." You'll feel you don't have enough information to even make an informed decision.

Set them anyway. These numbers help us prioritize, work harder, and allow us to plan long term.

Including deadlines and earnings for your Goals creates an intention. When you know you want to finish your book by the end of the year, you're more likely to push to reach that Goal. When you've committed to leaving your job by the end of the year but need to make a certain amount of money before you can quit, you're less likely to procrastinate and more likely to ask for higher rates for your work.

It's a learning process that grows with you and your writing career.

As you work on a project, you'll have a better idea of how long it will take. As you pitch for money, you'll quickly learn how much you can make. As you try new things to reach your Goals, you'll gain more insight into completing your Goals.

> *We need to talk about money.*
>
> *Too often, we shy away from discussing money when it comes to our dreams. We're artists, writers, dreamers, right? We want to create. Money shouldn't limit us.*
>
> *Let's be honest.*
>
> *While the life you most want to live won't have a core value of money, reality dictates we need money to live. We need to eat and have a solid roof under which we'll sleep in bed at night. If you want to realize your dream life, you'll need a certain amount of money to make that happen.*
>
> *Can you pay your mortgage? Your child's daycare? How much are your grocery bills each month? What about the extras, like new clothes, travel, and other luxuries?*
>
> *How much you need to live comfortably depends on where you live, how you live, and how many dependents you have. Including a specific number as a money Goal sets a clear yet achievable destination for your journey.*

Creating A Fourth Goal - Your Money Goal!

Yes, I know I said only three Goals, but a Money Goal is a little different. A Money Goal flows naturally from your other Goals and helps you outline how much you want to make from the work you plan to do. It won't create additional work but allows you to highlight your income streams and set money amounts for each stream.

Example of a Money Goal with money streams:

Objective: I want to become an expert in animal behavior and training, so I can make a living writing articles and books on my topics of expertise.

Money Goal: I want to make 100K/year.

- **Strategy One**: 25K/year selling articles on dog training.
- **Strategy Two**: 20K/year selling books.
- **Strategy Three**: 15K/year selling dog training courses online.
- **Strategy Four**: 40K/year speaking at dog training institutes and conferences.

Setting a dollar amount to your Goals also helps you view your other writing Goals as earning opportunities. When you know you want to make x-amount of money writing articles, you're likely to send out more pitches, ask for more money and push harder to reach that Goal.

Even more important, money dictates a tangible value for your work. Your Goal requires you to advocate for yourself and your work as you ask clients, editors, and publishers to pay you.

And don't you deserve to be paid for your work?

Yes. Absolutely. You do.

And now it's time to celebrate!!!!

"What?" you may be wondering. We're not done. We're only two letters into a four letter process. What is there to celebrate?

We're celebrating how much you've accomplished so far.

Always celebrate your wins, big and small. It's an important part of reaching your Objective.

You've just completed the two most daunting parts of the OGSM.

You know what you want and the kind of work you'll do. You've outlined your priorities. You've grappled with issues of money, rid yourself of things that weren't working for you, and also begun to visualize how you will create this inspiring life you want to live.

This is tough work. Don't let the moment pass without recognizing the good you've done. Whether working on an OGSM, cleaning your apartment, or writing a book, make a habit of giving yourself regular pats on the back.

There will always be more to do. You will always smack your head against challenges and frustrations. These moments of celebration remind us we are moving forward and, even more, who we are and what we have already done is enough.

So take a walk, enjoy chocolate, go camping, buy a new book to read, or schedule a massage. That new movie you've been wanting to see? Sneak out for a matinee and treat yourself with popcorn. Do whatever it is you want to do, as long as you take some time for you.

When you've done celebrating yourself, we'll get back to the Strategies section of our OGSM.

S IS FOR STRATEGY

GETTING DOWN TO THE NITTY GRITTY.

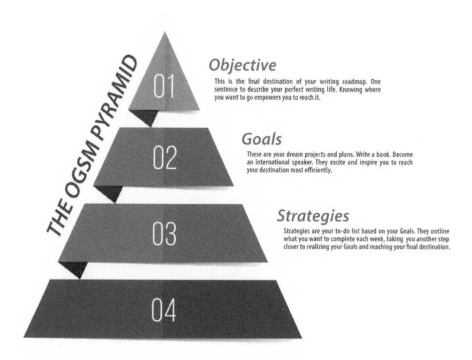

THE OGSM PYRAMID

01

Objective
This is the final destination of your writing roadmap. One sentence to describe your perfect writing life. Knowing where you want to go empowers you to reach it.

02

Goals
These are your dream projects and plans. Write a book. Become an international speaker. They excite and inspire you to reach your destination most efficiently.

03

Strategies
Strategies are your to-do list based on your Goals. They outline what you want to complete each week, taking you another step closer to realizing your Goals and reaching your final destination.

04

Remember the specific details I've been telling you to set aside as we've been working on your Objective and Goals? The ones I keep saying we'll get to later?

Now is their time.

Thinking again of that drive from New York to San Francisco. You know where you want to go and have a route planned. You've sketched an outline of what you want to do on the trip, and now, finally, you get to make choices that answer the what and how.

You'll decide where you'll stop just for the night and where you'll linger for longer. Do you want music and barbecue in Memphis or would you prefer hiking and camping in Colorado?

Strategies, simply put, are the processes and projects you'll complete that lead you to fulfill your Goals. They include the steps you will take to create products and services to gain the income you outline in your Goals.

Your Strategies are your active to-do list.

Since examples explain best, let's start there:

Objective: I want to become an expert in animal behavior and training, so I can make a living writing articles and books on my topic of expertise.

Goal One: I want to write and sell self-published books.
- **Strategy One**: Write The Parents' Guide to Buying A Dog.
- **Strategy Two**: Research places to self-publish.
- **Strategy Three**: Format book and create cover for completed book.

Goal Two: I want to be known as an expert in dog training.

- **Strategy One**: Pitch and write articles about dog training.
- **Strategy Two**: Submit proposals to speak at dog training institutes and conferences.
- **Strategy Three**: Create and sell online courses on dog training.

Goal Three: Make 25K/year writing and publishing articles.

- **Strategy One**: Write and pitch articles to regular magazines.
- **Strategy Two**: Research dog training magazines to pitch.

Notice, also, how Strategies can overlap with your Goals.

Writing and pitching articles, in particular, serves many purposes for your OGSM plan. You develop your expertise, make money, and build an audience.

As you develop the Strategies for your OGSM, you'll find other areas of overlap. It's wonderful when this happens because the individual actions you take and to-do list items you complete serve more than one purpose as you move you toward your Objective. It means less work with more benefit. Thus, you can focus on fewer Strategies with greater impact.

Outlining The Strategies For Your Goals

Remember back in the Goals section of this book, we separated your long list of potential projects into categories? I asked you to set them aside. Let's go back and get that original list of categories with their corresponding potential projects.

At this point:

- You've removed the things you no longer want to do.
- You've highlighted the work that pays your bills you'd like to phase out.
- You separated your top projects into categories.
- Then you chose the top three categories to be your Goals.

The projects under each of those Goal categories become your Strategies. You may want to tweak them a bit to make them feel like a clear to-do list or put them in the order that makes the most sense for you.

Some Goals will require very simple or very few strategies. Others are more complicated and include a series of steps to complete.

Goals with a simple strategy:

Goal: I want to support myself by writing freelance articles.

Strategy: Pitch articles until editors say yes. Then write those articles and be paid.

Goal: I want to write a book.

Strategy: Write 2 hours/day on my book.

Goals that incorporate multiple steps:

Goal: I want to build my writer's platform on social media.

- **Strategy One**: Choose the social media accounts you want to use.
- **Strategy Two**: Begin interacting with other writers through posts, photos, and shares.
- **Strategy Three**: Develop relationships with readers.

- **Strategy Four**: Develop relationships with other writers.

Goal: Create online course for copywriting
- **Strategy One**: Design Course.
- **Strategy Two**: Find best way to host course online.
- **Strategy Three**: Research ways to market online course.

The Ebb And Flow Of Strategies

Unlike Objective and Goals, Strategies change more often. As you complete a Strategy, you can cross it off your list and move onto the next. You may also find some Strategies don't work as you thought they would or you don't want to do them anymore. In both cases, you modify or remove the Strategy as it best fits your OGSM plan.

At the beginning of this book, I told you how my OGSM took me from confused and frustrated to living the exact writing life I yearned for but had no idea how to create. Let me walk you through my own OGSM and show you how my Strategies unfolded.

MY GOAL ONE:

Write and publish articles, short fiction, and short non-fiction.
- **Strategy One**: Set aside time each week to write.
- **Strategy Two**: Pitch articles to editors.

This Goal and its Strategies are ongoing. I am constantly writing and submitting my work for publication.

MY GOAL TWO:

Develop writing education products and services to sell online.

When I began, I prioritized my Strategies based on how quickly I could roll out the product or service as well as what resources I'd need to develop them.

- **Strategy One**: Set up The Workshop Online Writing Academy Group. (Done.)
- **Strategy Two**: Offer one-on-one mentoring sessions through my website. (Done.)
- **Strategy Three**: Host Creative Revolution Retreats international writing retreats for women. (Launched my first retreat in 2014 and more retreats coming)
- **Strategy Four**: Host annual Women's Writing Mentorship Exchange. (Launched first Mentorship Exchange in 2013. Continues yearly.)
- **Strategy Five**: Write and publish my OGSM Handbook. (Now!)
- **Strategy Six**: Research best ways to sell on my website. (Now!)
- **Strategy Seven**: Expand and develop The Workshop (Now!)
- **Strategy Eight**: Write the Rejection Handbook (TBD)
- **Strategy Nine**: Expand writing retreats to more countries and for additional demographics (TBD)

Keep in mind, when I first wrote my OGSM, I did not start with nine Strategies. That would have been madness. These Strategies evolved over the course of years.

I began by taking one-on-one clients and creating an online writing community because I could start them immediately. I already had the materials needed to set them in motion at hand and the teaching experience and technologies I needed to implement them.

Other Strategies, such as the international writing retreats and the books I write, take more time. Once my first two Strategies were well in motion, I began working on the first retreat and writing a book.

Your Strategies will rise organically, one from the other, as you do the work.

For example, in my work with clients online and in person, I saw certain issues repeatedly arise that demonstrated a clear need for this workbook and The Rejection Handbook. (Strategies Five and Eight.) Once I wrote the first book, I figured out how to publish it. (Strategy Six.)

As you implement your Strategies, you'll find what works best for you and what doesn't. This will help you refine each Strategy so you can improve your services, your products, and your writing. All of these things add to your expertise.

For example, once I had The Workshop running, had a solid list of one-on-one clients and began writing books and article, I realized I was doing too much. I stopped taking one-on-one clients and shifted my teaching focus to The Workshop, allowing me to work with more people and still have time to write.

Prioritizing Your Strategies

Strategies fall into three categories:

1. Those in progress.
2. Those that are new.
3. Those that you'll do one day in the future

In Progress Projects

I currently have three in progress Strategies for my education Goal.

1. Creative Revolution Writing Retreats.
2. My yearly Women's Writing Mentorship Program in which I match new writers with experienced writers for an hour of mentoring.
3. Further develop The Workshop to provide more value and be easier to run.

While they require consistent effort, they are already organized. I've done them before and have created processes to run them. They take much less time and guesswork than creating a new project from scratch.

Brand Spanking New Projects

When you first begin a Strategy, you're still learning how to manage it. It takes time to write a new book, design a new course, or pitch editors or copywriting clients.

Over time, you'll learn certain methods work better for you than others.

Let's say your goal is to make a living freelance writing, the more experience you have pitching, the more money you can ask for your pitches. Once you've pitched 20, 50, 100 times, you realize your pitches are solid, so you start asking for more money and pitching higher paying publications.

> **Pro-Tip: Ask for the money you're worth**
>
> *Many new writers are too nervous to ask for more money for their articles because they don't have confidence in their pitches. You don't have to wait for more experience to ask for more money for your work or to pitch higher paying publications. In fact, I suggest you start by aiming high. The worst that happens is you get a no and try somewhere else.*

Future Projects

Some Strategies have to wait for later.

You're back on your roadtrip. You'd love to see the Wisconsin Cheese House, but going there would take you days out of the way with little else to show for it, so you decide to forgo eating cheese because you'd rather see the Pacific Ocean.

I know I want to write a Rejection Handbook. I also have a memoir-based non-fiction book about pregnancy in progress. Not to mention some ideas I have for a science fiction YA novel in the works. One day I will fit them in, but for now, I have other priorities.

As you look forward to the next twelve months of your plan, you can plug your Maybe Projects into your timeline as they seem to fit. It's also possible you'll decide you don't want to do them because they don't fit your OGSM at all. These are the pieces of your plan that wait until you're ready.

Client Case Study

A woman came to me with a novel she was writing. She worked on it a bit here and there, but not really. After meeting with her a few times, it became clear she wasn't focused on the book at all.

This woman had other goals for her writing that took priority. She wanted to freelance as well as find more readers for her parenting blog. In her OGSM plan, her blog and freelancing brought money and sponsors. They paid her bills, supported her travel and established her as an expert at parenting and travel with kids.

We had many serious talks with her about her novel. Yes, she loves the idea of writing it, but in her bigger picture, it just didn't have a place.

Yet. It didn't have a place yet.

One day, she applied on a whim to a writing residency. She didn't think she had much of a chance, after all, she had no novel writing experience. Then she received her acceptance letter. You know what convinced the residency program to accept her? They loved her blog and specifically the work she had done supporting parents.

Your Maybe Projects can be a source of encouragement. When you look at the open space in front of you, anything is possible. You can write a book, pitch your biggest outlet yet, and publish a story that inspires millions. As you move them one at a time onto your OGSM, you will see them take color, shape, and form. Soon, they will become your accomplishments.

How Your Strategies Connect To Your Objective And Goals

I've mentioned how individual Strategies often support more than one Goal. My retreats and mentorship program are both education services that also set me up as an expert in writing. This book, in addition to educating, fulfills my desire to write and publish.

Each Strategy you include in your OGSM relates directly back to your Objective in some substantial way.

More real life client examples of how strategies support goals.

Goal: Become known as an expert in horseback riding, travel, and technology.
- **Strategy**: Pitch articles in my three expert subject areas.
- **Strategy**: Pitch a column for a national horseback riding magazine.
- **Strategy**: Take a year to travel around the United States visiting horseback riding ranches.

Each of these three Strategies directly fulfills the above Goal. They also help this writer make a living and help her reach her publishing Goal.

Goal: I want to phase out my current work and make 75K/year and support myself with freelance writing.
- **Strategy One**: Find 5 new copywriting clients that pay 500USD/month each.
- **Strategy Two**: Pitch editors and be paid for my articles.
- **Strategy Three**: Find new places to find writing work.

You can see how each Strategy of this goal separates into a discrete income stream, thus addressing her income goal along with developing her expertise and publishing.

But what if what you want to do something you've never done before?

It is likely your OGSM will include to-dos you've never done before. What if it requires learning a new skill? Or spending money on education? Or jumping feet first into something without any guarantee of a positive outcome? All of this can be frightening and overwhelming.

I have two pieces of advice for you here.

The first and most important: trust yourself.

Let me repeat that again.

Trust in yourself and your abilities.

What if there's something you don't know how to do? You can learn. You can research. You can ask questions. You can take a class. You can find the support you need to do whatever it is you want to do.

Believe me, I know. I was petrified at the idea of starting a retreat. Who would come? I don't know how to do marketing. How am I going to plan an event? I have no experience with that.

It turns out, I do have plenty of experience planning trips. After all, I spent years traveling full time with my family. I know how to find contacts in other countries and set up a place to stay. I've learned how to find the resources I need wherever I go, and my retreat participants benefit from my experience. It doesn't matter that I don't have specific hospitality experience. I figured it out and so will you.

The second piece of advice? Don't sell yourself short by telling yourself you're not good at something. Instead, think of how you can parlay what you know into a writing career you love.

The Mother of All Examples: Writing a book.

I have yet to meet someone who has full confidence in her ability to write a book before she writes it. More often than not, I hear excuse after excuse, reason after reason for why it may not happen.

But writing a book is like any other endeavor you undertake. If you keep working at it, if you keep moving forward, you will get where you are going.

Now, take some time to connect your Strategies to your Goals.

- YOUR ANSWERS HERE -

- YOUR ANSWERS HERE -

- YOUR ANSWERS HERE -

As you're working hard on fulfilling your Strategies and achieving your goals, you'll hit setbacks, and you'll make mistakes. People will say no. E-mails will go unanswered, and you'll sometimes find yourself frustrated. You didn't think it would be entirely without challenges, did you?

When you hit those inevitable rough spots on the road, you'll question yourself. As you implement each Strategy, you'll wonder if your plan is actually working.

Which brings us to the final section of The Writer's Roadmap.

Measures.

M IS FOR
MEASURES

PULLING OUT YOUR RULER

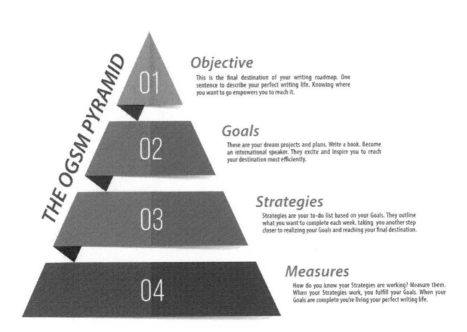

THE OGSM PYRAMID

01 *Objective*
This is the final destination of your writing roadmap. One sentence to describe your perfect writing life. Knowing where you want to go empowers you to reach it.

02 *Goals*
These are your dream projects and plans. Write a book. Become an international speaker. They excite and inspire you to reach your destination most efficiently.

03 *Strategies*
Strategies are your to-do list based on your Goals. They outline what you want to complete each week, taking you another step closer to realizing your Goals and reaching your final destination.

04 *Measures*
How do you know your Strategies are working? Measure them. When your Strategies work, you fulfill your Goals. When your Goals are complete you're living your perfect writing life.

Measures are exactly as they sound. They measure whether or not your Strategies are working.

Implementing a plan requires resources. The gas in our tanks. The money in our pockets, and the amount of time we can spend in a car each day before we're sick of sitting there.

That's why we need measures. To keep us honest. So we can figure out if we're spending our money wisely or wasting gas when getting needlessly lost.

You'll also notice this Measures section is short and sweet. They are easy to set and quickly help you determine the efficacy of your Strategies.

Do you want to make a certain amount of money? That's your Measure. You're either hitting your income goal, or you're not.

Do you want to send a specific number of pitches every month? Another Measure. You either send them, or you don't.

While you can question whether or not your chosen Strategy is the best method to reach your Goal, you cannot argue with a cold hard number. You either meet your Measure, or you don't.

Two Ways To Set Your Measures

You can set a specific number that relies entirely on the work you put into a project and isn't dependent on receiving a response from someone else.

Such as:
I will send out 20 pitches per month.
Or
I will send a query to 30 new potential clients.
Or

I will write for thirty minutes every morning before the kids get up.

Whether or not you meet your Measures rests entirely on you, which means you don't have to rely on anyone else to fulfill them. You have total control.

The second way to set your measures is to focus on the outcome of your actions.

For example:
I will publish in 2 new publications/month.
Or
I will find 12 new copywriting clients this year.
Or
I will make 500 dollars more income this month than last month.

These rely on others to say yes or no. If you don't get the yeses you still need to satisfy the measure, so you buckle down and send more queries and pitches.

What to expect when pitching editors or finding clients.

When pitching editors, even the most successful writer with well-developed editorial contacts only gets yeses fifty percent of the time. When you're new and cold pitching, expect that number to drop to something more like twenty percent.

If you're cold pitching clients looking for copywriting or other work, that number plunges further to 5-10%.

This is not to discourage you, but to give you a benchmark against which you can evaluate the success of your Strategies. If you send 5 pitches a month, and only find 1 new client in three months, you're actually doing quite well. But if you want more clients, you need to send more letters.

If you're pitching only once a week and never, ever get a single response from an editor, it could be the pitch. It could also be over the course of 6 weeks, you've only sent six pitches. That's not enough information to know if your pitches need tweaking. Instead, pitch more often if you want to publish more.

If however, you find you're not getting the results you want no matter how much you put yourself out there, then it's time to tweak the Strategy. Are you sending your letters to the right type of clients? Does your letter communicate what you want potential clients to hear? Are you spending enough time per week working on your Goal or are you procrastinating and getting distracted?

How To Set The Number Of The Measure

A measure can be the percentage of a project you complete, the number of pages you write, pitches you send, clients you query, or the dollar amount you earn.

Are you hitting your money goals? Are you writing enough pages? Are you moving forward toward your Strategies in a way that will meet deadlines and ultimately your Goals? It's a simple yes or no answer.

The numbers you set may feel arbitrary the first time you set your measures. If you haven't pitched editors, how do you know how many to send per month to reach your income goals? Make an educated guess. As you begin pitching and working with editors, you'll see what works for you and what doesn't. Then you'll refine your Measures to better fit your plan.

- YOUR ANSWERS HERE -

- YOUR ANSWERS HERE -

How Long Do You Wait To Decide Your Strategies Aren't Helping You Meet Your Goals?

This depends on your Strategy and Measure.

If you include a Measure to write ten pages on your book or send 20 pitches a month and you're not writing or sending, you don't need much time to know why you're not meeting your Measure.

It's pretty clear in this case, you need to write and pitch more.

Other measures -- such as finding 10 new copywriting clients -- take longer.

It is notoriously difficult to find copywriting clients when you first begin. Statistics I've heard? For every twenty queries you send, you may find one new client. So if you've sent 50 pitches and only have three new clients, it can feel like you're not reaching your Goals when really you're comfortably within the range of normal acceptance.

Or it's easy to conclude there's something wrong with your book when you send it to five potential agents and all of them say "Not for me!" But agents say no for all kinds of reasons that have nothing to do with you or your book, and five agents isn't a large enough sample by which to judge. Many writers query tens of agents before finally finding the right one for them.

If your Measures continue to fall short of the mark month after month with no forward movement, then it's time to look at your Strategies and examine what's going on. Do your pitches include the right information? Are you submitting to the right journals? Are you looking in the right place for clients? Are you offering potential clients what they actually need? Is your book blurb too long? Is your cover not right for your genre? Does your book need another edit before plunging back into the agent and publisher pool?

If you don't know? Ask people you trust, because no one has expertise in all areas. We all need support and feedback.

Find a group of other writers, join a mastermind writing group, or hire a marketing professional to help you on your way. Find a trusted reader to comment on your book. Sometimes even a quick consult with an expert can answer simple questions that can entirely change the way you run your writing business.

This brings us to the end of the last section of your OGSM. You've defined your Objective. You now know what you want from your writing. You've highlighted your main Goals and outlined the Strategies that will support them. All that, and you have Measures that will help you evaluate your Strategies to make sure they're working.

Now what?

You have a plan! Now it's time for action!

Congratulations once again!

You've made it all the way to the end of your writer's journey.

You began with a blank page and questions, and now you have a clear roadmap to take you from where you are now to where you want to go. This plan includes your big fat hairy dreams broken down into smaller parts you can add to your weekly to do lists.

Now it's time for you to start writing, pitching, and creating. Implement the Strategies you laid out and watch them grow to fulfill your Goals. As you reach your goals, you'll suddenly notice you're closer than you ever believed to living your ideal writing life.

But you're not quite finished with your OGSM or this book.

Each month, go back and check your OGSM. Read through and reevaluate based on your last month of work.

What's working for you?

What's not?

Are there parts of your OGSM that no longer fit?

Are you finding you're doing too much and feeling overwhelmed?

Modify, shift, and change the parts that don't serve you, while you continue to focus on the parts of your OGSM that inspire you to keep moving forward.

Again, don't worry if it doesn't feel 100% yet. Everyone feels wobbly when they begin to implement their first OGSM.

Day by day, a week at a time, then over the course of months, you will watch your career grow. You will write, publish, and begin to make a living through your work. You'll break away from all the things you don't want and let go of what holds you back as you ride the road you designed for yourself.

While I can't promise a specific outcome from your OGSM -- that depends entirely on you --, I can say if you start your plan now, you'll see your Strategies come to life which will lead directly to your Goals. When you reach your Goals, you'll look around and realize you are living your life's Objective.

Start today. Start now and imagine where you will be one year from now.

It will be amazing.

ABOUT THE
AUTHOR

Hello! I'm Leigh Shulman, writer, teacher and mentor.

I remember the first time I sat down to write. I was about 12, flooded with raging hormones and super pissed at my parents (basically like all twelve-year-olds) but instead of acting out, I pulled out a pen and paper and put my feelings on the page. I was hooked!

In college, I discovered I loved teaching creative writing, almost as much as I loved the writing itself. I went on to earn an MA in Creative Writing and Education from the City College of NY. I dreamt of spending my days writing, teaching, and exploring the world.

But life doesn't quite work like that.

I ended up working as a web producer for MTV. While I enjoyed what I did, it was an insanely stressful job, and I found it nearly IMPOSSIBLE to find the time to write. Then, when my first daughter Lila was born, my writing ground to a halt.

If you have kids, I'm sure you get it. I was tired, irritable, and super distracted, not exactly fertile ground for inspiration. Plus, I was worried no one wanted to hear what I had to say anymore, that I didn't have any more creativity to give. It got to the point where every area of my life took priority over my writing. As I lost sight of my goals and passion, my confidence nearly disappeared.

I wrote this in my journal when Lila was one-year-old.

If I keep going the way I've been going, I will never do the things I want to do. I will never travel. I will never write. I will never create what I want in my life.

#TRUTH

Fortunately, I turned that ship around. My family and I sold everything we owned and traveled the world for three years! We lived in Europe, Panama, and finally settled in Argentina. During this time I taught writing wherever we ventured, and I found ways to work writing back in my life.

My confidence blossomed, my inspiration grew, and my work benefited in quality and quantity. I had never felt like more of a badass.

Fast forward ten years. My work has been featured in The New York Times, The Huffington Post, The Guardian, The Establishment, Guernica, Mashable, and many other publications. I've published two books I'm incredibly proud of and have taught at Barnard College, CUNY, Yeshiva University, the Brooklyn Academy of Music, and countless other programs.

I seriously couldn't be happier.

Now, I spend my time running The Workshop, my online academy for people who want to make money with their words and teaching at amazing writing retreats because I want to help more women feel confident with their writing, finish their masterpieces, and build professional careers!

This is why I'm so excited you've picked up this book. I want to show you, without a doubt, you are strong, wonderful, and creative. I want to show you why you can write and absolutely must share what you have to say with the world.

It's hard knowing what you want from your writing and even harder to make it happen.

That's why I'm here.

To offer you the tools and encouragement to make your writing dreams come true.

For free writing resources, courses and more, sign up for updates here: http://bit.ly/leighshulman

70007077R00064

Made in the USA
Columbia, SC
19 August 2019